THE MALTESE DREAMBOOK

By Gabriel Levin

GABRIEL LEVIN

The Maltese Dreambook

ANVIL PRESS POETRY

ACKNOWLEDGEMENTS

Some of the poems and translations in this collection have
appeared in *Ariel, The Jerusalem Review, Oasis, Parnassus,
PN Review, Princeton University Library Chronicle ,
Raritan* and the *Times Literary Supplement.*

Published in Great Britain in 2008
by Anvil Press Poetry
Neptune House 70 Royal Hill London SE10 8RF

ISBN 978 0 85646 409 6

This book is published with financial assistance
from Arts Council England

Set in Monotype Janson by Anvil
Printed in Great Britain
by The Cromwell Press Trowbridge Wiltshire

A catalogue record for this book
is available from The British Library

for Boaz

Contents

Under Cedar Skies

THE NUMEN

You had gone on about sudden windfalls
tumbling into our laps unbeknown and timely
like stabs of sunlight in winter as I slipped
in my pocket a snapshot of an old Underwood tongued
with fire that you'd dug out of your drawer,
and we spoke of what it meant to be a rhapsode
(the lit stub in your hand skirting the precincts
of your body) while minutes before our words had woven
the strangest notions: my battered portable,
we agreed, had turned into an instrument
of the archaic, and you fancied time had stripped the space
we inhabit to a point where silence reigned,
as words in the absence of a foothold shriveled
to nothing. And the mind quivered to pour
its contents freely as a raft threading the river
we'd come to accept in time as our own.

VIGIL

The log flared on the grate
as I poked its side, poor demon

left to its own devices, hissed
blue lipped, then shriveled

into itself like a stunned
worm, before turning to ashes;

I stirred in my chair, half conscious
of darkness lapping –

even you, my lambent fawn, soft
hammered in copper,

leapt back into the shadows
of the holy mountain

(whose rock makes us fierce)
with nothing to confess

when I rose without ceremony
and called it a night.

A CAPPELLA

He was no more than knee high
when his father jiggled the door off its hinges
and laid it flat between two chairs
as a makeshift table for the unbidden
guests that night, who clapped with joy before digging in,
but he swore all changed in the mind
of the child he barely outgrew: here was the given
he would seek for how many years
and score in the bark of poetry.

The city in a festive mood greets
the rhapsode whose words plumb the length
of his body and stamp the soil
of Sion, a crusty hill that bellows like a lion smelted
in Solomon's mines,
                              its name pointing
to itself, bookish index finger or signpost
for the strangers we conjure up
and summon to feast under the terebinth
when the day grows hot; the tale
shadows our lives even to the present, and turns
into a tune dropped in our ears
by the soot-headed bulbul in the foliage:
Stay your heart, stay your heart.

                    *

Looking up I saw them standing
near me, dear ones I might have counted
on my fingers as they disentangled themselves
from the family tree
                              and stooped their shoulders

to the burden: one collapsed at a burning door,
coated in the cinders of a language seeded with hope,
while another rose daily to temper
beauty with glancing blows (*la belle feuille
mordorée*) – and whose words
if not yours, old ghost, siren on the bare rock
of conscience? These are the fathers
bedded down in memory.

So we broke bread, and our eyes
uncorked, delighting in the cloister bloom
and imagined mater Genetrix abandoning her perch
on the high walls to soft-pedal the air above us;
then we fell silent, hung fire at the door, timidly alert –
    like hares
on the run – before stepping out of our lump
selves, and hovering nave high,
unfledged, incomplete, risen among winged
creatures of a different order.

SLEEPER IN THE WADI

after Rimbaud

It's a green hollow where a spring gushes
and giddily snags on cane its silver
tatters; where the sun, from its proud crest,
shimmers: it's a wadi lathered in rays.

A young recruit, slack-jawed, bare-headed,
neck awash in blue sprays of cress,
naps; at ease in the grass, under wisps of cirrus,
pale in his green bedding where light rains.

Toes curled in swordgrass, he sleeps. Smiling
as a sick child might smile, he dozes:
Cushion him warmly, earth: he's caught a chill.

The scent of thyme doesn't tease his nostrils;
he sleeps in the sun, fist on his chest
undisturbed. Two red holes in his side.

XENOS

I

He who stood on the far side of the reed bank
while I took note of his mangled

shadow, spoke to us of the past contrafactual.
Phrases flew by like buckshot

but I only managed to catch a single word,
apodosis, as I waded towards him.

I lifted his frail body, crippled
the waist down, in my arms

and bore him to the hither side of the incredulous,
following my own lights, as it were.

2

Weeks later, traveling fast from zones
of darkness into light

I work my way back from the dream residue
and tenor of things flung together

and lodged in the promise, *the eye that gazes
on me will not see me*, as if the quest

had come to this, the end clause
harboring nothing but its own sinuous

inconclusiveness, the self sliced
lengthwise like a flatfish, for ever.

SAFFURIYA

for Taha Muhammad Ali

The ruin of his village was the single spot where memory
might be sown, and when the cinders and stones
were cleared, and the earth tapped open like a Byzantine
    jewel box,
the wistful face of a woman from the Galilee
smiled softly out of the dust, and whispered, "Go on."
And so he set out not as vagabond prince
across the twisted dunes, but a wily gamester,
who'd found just the right spin to put on words.
One moment the land stared back at him with the eyes of
    a kid goat,
the next of a hyena, and like the brigand
on the run in the *Book of Songs,* he put his ear to the ground
and heard men's hearts beating beneath his feet.

A DREAM OF CRETE

Over the stepping stones in single file
down the sheer corridor where *kri-kri*
slip in and out of sight, disgorged onto a shingle beach
we might have been so many adorants,
lump figurines in lost wax promptly restored to light
as we raised hands to shield our eyes,
dead on our feet, out of season
itinerants on the bright shore.

One amphora of honey, for Our Lady
of the Labyrinth, a flock of wethers bred for wool
and must from the vine stock: lost parts
of speech fired in argil. October gusts
send the spume singing across the tamarisk bay
as its tattered cryptogram unravels
where I stand. Who was it claimed long
sleep and dream his only teacher?

Berthed in the *Lissos* bound for the mainland
a poltergeist of soft-talking knocks
and groans in the strongbox cabin soothe the mind,
loath to relinquish the thread of a path
fathoms above the cove whose name
now ships me home, or birdsong in tesserae
and a door kicked open onto shadow
lives washed in magenta.

LINES IN AMORGOS

What of the figure in the craft slumped
in the stern, his features crumpled by the tightening vice

of nightfall? The outboard sputters across the bay
and scribbles its own leucocholic scrawl

till he kills the engine and leans overboard.
Someone snaps and billows in my face a paper tablecloth

with a map of the island, while the man
looping the loop in the waters of Katapola sails in and docks

in front of my table. "Barracuda," the waiter
whispers to me as the boatman silently slaps his catch

on the glowing plate of the outdoor grill,
though I swear I can't tell if he's referring to the fish

or the man of baleful demeanor. Weaving
between tables he accompanies with a cracked voice

snatches of song that spill out of the taverna
for a night and a day. *Let go of the prey*

for the shadow, I murmur into the chewed off ears
of the cat who's slinked under my chair –

but the clenched fist unclenches nothing
from its grip. And I squint at the prick of lights

on the other side of the bay, where patient Erato sits
with a lyre on faux marble knees,

chipped and white as votive idols sent over the seas,
or the plainer cuttlebone on the shore.

PAPYRI

Orphaned page where the eye
lip-reads scraps too small and ragged
to illumine the mind for long: rank and file figures
of speech stamping their feet in the cold
as they breathe into hands I'd like to take into mine;
word-stems spirited away and retrieved
in the lee of brackets, but only as conjecture
between ellipses where blank seraphs
lie low ... *and of the kindly Goddesses ... beneath*
the misty darkness ... of speech ... my ear,
pressed numbly against your phantasmal yield,
tingles for a moment with unknowing,
a quicksilver darkness that won't let me go
when I wake slumped over my desk;
don't ask how come I'm fumbling now
for words, riffling through your scattered lexis –
auriferous idiom, pitch and ambit,
plain speech or idiolect I've stumbled on,
don't draw the line as I linger here, scraping
my knees where your scent trails off.

SAMBATYON

And ink is the name of your spirit
— ABULAFIA

Even as the flux swelled and rushed headlong
he stared hard at the furious script
of foam, and could have sworn someone had tripped
and scattered the alphabet into the strong
brew of gravel and sand that left him short
of breath, and threw him for a loop, as he bared
his heart to the white waters that flared
and ripped a window to the mind's retort.
Now he could move on into the open
field, heaven knows how a free fall of words
rained from the skies, or was it a roll-
call of molten sounds that rose unchosen
from his lips – truly a language for the birds,
a tongue lashed to the river's scroll.

Dwindling on the Sabbath to a crawl
the river that swallowed its tongue, absurd
as it sounds, now beckoned to us from the cloven
banks, we who'd never seen its scrawl
(and of the unbinding of the soul hadn't heard)
knew only of the influx of a few chosen
words that tinkered with the mind for sport.
But when the bolts shot back, no one prepared
us for the light that poured in – a shared
vision furrowed the air, a wrongheaded sort
of rightness that might end in song
shook us to the core as we jumped and skipped
across the riverbed, enthusiasts tricked
out as magi, though not for long.

ARION

When the dolphin swept you up
from under, finning shoreward,
it *understood*, as in: to bear up, or seize

as in: "he was lifted, and a cloud
took him out of their sight."
At times a wind whisks the sea

into a froth and leaves us longing
for some all-encompassing fisheye
or stealthy zoom to steady our gaze –

but surely the brightest notions
are slow to dawn on any face
when the journey has come to this.

Pulled under by the deadweight
of your finery, you gagged on
a mouthful of song as unlooked for

relief sheared the sonar waves.

UNDER CEDAR SKIES

And the earth blinkered in its turning
and the seafront glowed like a pine torch in its dying,

and the little boats chugged out from Joppa,
past Andromeda's Rock, and clawed at the depleted sea

and the flying squadrons rumbled home from their raids
in your cedar skies, and the villagers huddled

in their clothes of trembling. – Oh, Antipater of Sidon,
who will sing in the rubble, "My love stumbled

and I fell"? Will you ever lay a forgiving (funerary) hand
on my shoulder? You who wrote of the ruins

of another city torn by war, most unhappy of ports
where the keening kingfishers alone remained

to scour the shoreline. I catch sight of them,
skirting the breakwater, intact, temperate birds.

The Maltese Dreambook

He touched the ochre spirals on the wall,
the oculus spirals of the Lady of Malta.

Costigan

THE MALTESE DREAMBOOK

I could almost believe you'd stepped
out of the oracle hole to greet me, doffing your beret
in my holiday poem, a shadowy sort
of thing, Pierrot, say, in an old coat
loitering on Gozo. A place to lie low for ever
so long.
        I had set off early in the morning,
tramping out past the bird-trapper hides,
and had lost my head over the prickly pear
and wayside convolvulus,
legions of snails creeping up the gangly fennel
(so many spirals to contend with)
when up you popped, *light as a blessed*
ghost,

        the sort of remark you might have made,
sailing into Valletta, and not STC fresh off the *Speedwell:*
"You can walk no where without having whispers
of Suicide, toys of desperation."
You smiled, Silky, from ear to ear
and led me by the elbow round the temple,
lobed like the ace of clubs, your spectral limestone
home, all buttery yellow – a soft place
to go down into,
                you and the black-banded grasshoppers
raveled into the Giant's Tower, its strapping,
rude slabs an antediluvial haven in-the-round, ovoid,
plump as the chiseled Fat Ladies behind glass
with replaceable trick-puppet
heads.

One such Lady lies on her side –
right hand under her head, ballooning hips,
a pleated skirt exposing tiny
overburdened trotters – dozing, or better,
dreaming, as I had, on my very first night in Malta,
of assorted fruits borne in a string bag
for a family in need, the dreamscape neither light
nor dark, my bearings lost, I wander
into the home of strangers who wolf down the windfall
in gratitude,
                   while for the Sleeping Lady
the archipelago is swaddled in a sedimentary
dream of its own genesis: a deep marine ooze of skeletal
    deposits
that harden to stone and surge from the sea
in scarps and faults, blue clay slopes
and high, nascent grounds.

               *

Bingo night on Triq Republica.
The streets so narrow and steep
it's a tumble to the tip of the promontory.
I step out of The Shipwrecked
to follow the bobbing Sultana down
Merchant Street, eight burly Maltese
keeping the fairy queen afloat, a double row
of children treading in her wake,
rounding the block behind the standard bearers
and the monstrance, parents blowing kisses
at their little ones, sweet buns in hand,
as I wander off to my lodgings
– and in the early hours
of the morning I flee the city,
a child in my arms, glancing back

at the tripwire explosions, one building
after another collapsing behind us, *not proud,*
just lucky I jot down upon waking and call
to mind photographs of the blanket
bombing I'd gazed at in the Bibliotheca,
Valletta reduced to a dust-heap.

*

Comino – small as a cumin
seed – lying midway
between the two larger
islands, where A,
("who razes the dwelling
and builds the ruin")
had fled from city to
city, and place to place,
until he reached *Cumtina*
and there dwelled against
his will for many days
along with the migrating
birds, and saw wonders
and composed the *Book*
of the Sign, here, where
the low, hanging valley runs
into St. Nicholas Bay,

with its trace of a redoubt
and chaste trees, and dark
kidney vetch, I open *Sefer*
Ha'Ot, and read: and YHWH
spoke to me when I saw
His name writ in blood
and unique in my heart
sorting out blood from ink

and ink from blood
and YHWH said to me
see your soul's name is
blood and ink is the name
of your spirit, and see
how your father and mother
long for this name
and this title of mine.

And hearing of the great
rift between soul
and spirit I thrilled
with joy, for I knew
my soul dwelled under
its own color in the mirror
red as blood, and that
my spirit dwelled under
its own color in the mirror
black as ink, and there raged
a war in my heart between
the blood and the ink,
and the blood was of air
and the ink of dust,
and the ink routed
the blood and the Sabbath
overpowered all the days
of the week, and my heart
was soothed, and I praised
YHWH with my mouth.

*

I shut the *Book of the Sign*, and shaking out a cramp
in my leg, circled the island half-expecting
to run into a solitary walker who would strike a chord

in my heart of hearts, as A might have said, and clapping
    my eyes
on the stranger I'd see an image of my own self,
but the dirt path only brought me to derelict farmhouses
and on the headland a turreted watch tower
commanding the straits, built by the Grand Master
whose portrait C had executed with typical
bravura – tatinium highlight gleaming off the armor
    plating –
soon after landing in Malta, a fugitive from Rome,
his life in mounting disorder, even friends
confessing to his oddness, his *stravagantissimo*
– he'd fatally stabbed a local tough in a street brawl
and wandered from the Alban Hills to Naples,
boarded a galley for the fortress island,
though not before leaving behind his darkest
Neapolitan paintings in the "new manner of that terrible
style of shadowing," as De Domenici wrote:
"the truth of those nudes, the resounding lights
without many reflections, stunned not only the dilettantes
but most of the practitioners." Haughty, restless
quick-tempered, he sought in Malta, if not a life
of virtue, then at least a knighthood that might bring
a papal pardon, as *The Beheading* smoothed the way
to his donning, briefly, the Order's habit.

*

Santa Maria Bay. Moiré ripple and spark under the street
lamp at the end of a small jetty. Silvery fish in droves skim
the surface for crumbs. Gleam of their scales as they flash
by in a phalanx. The nocturnal swaying of white, trumpet-
ed algae. A's "music of pure thought," lucid, insightful,
abstruse – in constant motion. His inner battle: rational and
imaginative thought – ink and blood, image and likeness –

and their convergence in his vision of the Man. I can't get
out of my mind the young woman's lightning fingers over
the keyboard in Valletta's tiny Manoel Theater. Her intent,
utter surrender to Schumann as she bent over the Steinway.
Willowy, in a scarlet dress, radiant as she rose to take her
bow. To believe this and let all else go …

*

A paean to the garrigue with its spiny shrubs
in pockets of soil here and there in the pockmarked
limestone along the coast: an aromatic karstland

of thyme and spurge, of heath and the olive-leaved
germander, secreting their oils like sunscreen
against the summer droughts and Levanter winds,

a paean to erosion and collapse, to sinkholes
and dolines shaped by percolating groundwater,
to caverns hollowed by pummeling waves,

and the drilling of tunnels and azure windows
for bathers to gaze through, and the swifts –
do they truly sleep in flight? – to scythe through.

*

It's a mongrel tongue they speak here
you whisper in my ear as I step off the old diesel
bus in Rabat. A laissez-faire Arabic
with its own Levantine gloss.
                              Muse of a string
in your phantasmal boots, won't you thread together
your scattered atoms for a friend?

The sun shines over the citadel with such ferocity
as I circle the walls. Barley stacked
on the stubble slopes, and then the high cliffs
where you'll string along with me (if only
I insist).

And STC "accounting to Conscience
For the Hours of every Day" wrote
in his journal:

A flash of Lightning/struck terror into my Heart – yea
– as if spiritual Things, *Beings of Thought* (Entia Rationis)
could cloath themselves & make a *space* of Light – the
Shekinah of the Conscience/ –
I seemed to see *my actions* in my mind/or my mind
seemed to have inclosed *that light* within its enlarged
Circumference/ – It was real & spectral at the same
moment/ – These are the *Ideas*/a cave, night, the Thunder
& Lightning & the guilty man/had been a Banditto, &
drank & caroused but yet never killed his sensibility – but
drugged it &c &c &c –

*

Hadn't he been on the run as well? His fell-walking
    and fantastic schemes, the prodigality
of his mind overshadowed by opium flights,
    a floundering marriage, bodily grievances that left him
                                        prostrate,
indolent, and, as he wrote, rudderless,
    but in the end driven to thoughts of fleeing
to Montpellier, America, the Azores, the West Indies –
    anywhere, his covert love for Sara H. pitched
him into a fervor he couldn't countenance, and so,
                                        writing to Wordsworth

of his "wish to retire into stoniness and to stir not,"
he landed, after an arduous sea voyage, in the remote
                                                    outpost
    of Malta

          (von Riedesel, 1773: *Reprefent to yourfelf a barren
and hard rock, where the upper-cruft has been beaten off,
pounded, and by moiftening it with water
converted into foil, which the indefatigable inhabitants
cultivate.)

          newly wrested from the French,
where the work of self-amendment began,
    and, as the Governor's affable Public Secretary
by day, he lived more truthfully
    belabyrinthed in the pages of his notebooks.

                    *

Squat, slit-windowed, tin-roofed hideaways,
large enough for a man to sit on his heels
and peer into the dawn – you, Silky, would
have found comfort here, waiting for the songbirds
to alight on rows of knee-high limestone blocks
fronting the hut, waiting to spring a net

on the songsters: it's cozy inside, a bird trapper forgot
his thermos and there's a moldy leather belt
dangling from a nail, better than any promenade,
any meander along the precipices, better than
squinting down the blowhole cleft dubbed
Mouth of the Pigeons, with a wind at your back.

                    *

What does it signify this medley of song
in the scrub? An array of flight-calls zit-zit-zit
and high-pitched scratch notes. Passerines

in their passagings. Chirps and scare notes,
chatter and microtones, snatches of melody,
pauses and iterations, a flock of warblers

gabbing on the wing, their flight low, undulant
back-circling, and is that – glissando –
a duet? Walking along the edge of the cliff

a jingle of notes funnels up from a leafy niche
in the rockface, half way down to the sea, *bloc
sonore,* crystalline, a fluent sound-world.

*

The figures stand life-size sinewed in light in the penum-
bra of the jailhouse courtyard. I can still picture them clus-
tered in a semi-circle. On the far left the servant girl in
profile, leaning forward, an empty gold platter in her out-
stretched hands, light glinting off the rim, curling around
her earlobe, her expression a touch impassive, or is it sup-
pressed shock on a face that resembles the face of the
angel in the *Flight into Egypt.* A step away to her left an eld-
erly woman in a black robe and shawl raises her hands in
horror to her face abraded like the field stones littering the
island. She has seen enough. The same light filtering down
from the upper left corner glances off her brow and gray
hair. At the apex of the semi-circle stands the bearded jail-
er, his hair closely cropped, a ring of keys jangling against
his thigh. Sporting a bottle-green cloak, he is pointing at
the platter. His is the voice we imagine hearing. The dark
command at the gate. Every morning as I entered the

Oratory to gaze at *The Beheading* my eye would track from the jailer's index finger, to the platter and then to the figure lying trussed on the floor between the executioner's spread-eagled legs. According to Bellori, C "worked with much fervor," using transparent glazes of brown that allowed for the dark priming to show through. What went on in *his* head as he painted the figure stooped over the Evangelist? C, who had lived his own life to the hilt, thrust into the hand of the handsome, bare-breasted executioner a dagger – perhaps the same blade that C kept under his pillow at night – with which to sever John the Baptist's head, for the tableau vivant is enacted in the breath pause, the briefest duration between the first swift blow of the sword (lying on the floor, if I'm not mistaken, at the furthest point from the source of light) that has sliced through the jugular without actually lopping off the head, the brutal wrenching of matter and spirit. The slayer, firmly planted opposite the servant girl – they could be bowing to each other in obeisance – bends down for the final coup de grace, white lead highlighting the edge of the dagger drawn behind his back, his left arm ramrodded against the martyr's head. Poor lighting and the distance from the huge canvas – it hangs recessed behind an altar – makes it almost impossible to see clearly, let alone remember, John's mask-like features. Is he serene, or merely drained of life, muted, earthbound, and untranslated? What I do remember are the loosened folds of the crimson mantel around his loins, exposing torso and legs in a darkness with nothing but the faintest light feathering his toes. And a tiny, triangular puddle of blood beneath his mouth where C has scrawled in red *f. michel: f* for frère, Michel the name he was given at birth.

*

A farmhouse all to myself tonight,
arrowhead layout of village along a high ridge –
terraced fields, dovecote tower, dip
and swell of a zigzagging path, muffled

bells, however far I stray, a sort
of sing-along dingdong, a winged semi-
quaver flits in the low brambles
and I'm down on my knees

as today's mock lepidopterist:
Adonis blue and creamy beige
with an orangey fringe when it folds
its wings, stock-still, on a twig –

walk on, past crumbling walls
cacti, a dry watercourse eating
into limestone, bare tract at land's
end, wind-gouged, mushroom

boulders, and closer to the edge
someone is leaning over the lip
of the cliff, it's a thirty-floor drop
to the cut-glass sea, he mumbles

to himself as he peers down, I creep up
then back, dizzy from the sight, *whispers*
of Suicide, and discern barely visible tackle
plunging into brine, hauled up one at

a time, a dripping hoop at the end
of each line, sunlight glinting off
scales of his catch, so I circle back –
trip over mop-headed squill bulbs

past a pillbox chapel, stunted salt trees,
fireworks factory DANGER scrawled red,
cylindrical dynamite sticks handled
with the loving care of a Torah scroll –

slog on, past weather-eaten stone
torsos rising out of tongues of fire, *Triq tal-Virtù*
and it is a hard bed to stretch out on
tonight in a farmhouse all to myself

*

Twice-told call notes bore into my sleep, insistent
birdsong dissolving the dream: someone
is bumped off (but *who?*), and puzzling over the details
becomes part of the mystery. I have a vague
recollection of chaperoning an eccentric
deranged family, teens left in my care,
siblings, and *snap* everything's gone awry:
there's a body to be disposed of – soundlessly,
behind closed doors. Hadn't I scribbled down
in the snackbar my own stray thoughts on *The Beheading?*
The two figures leaning forward at opposite ends
of an invisible arc: his brute expediency,
her grace and solicitude, heart beating fast
moments before the gruesome act. Where might she rest
her eyes if not on the platter? In a matter of seconds,
the head in her care, she will feel its tug
as she delivers the dish to her mistress
and retreats from view, the voice, *his* voice in her ears.
Could this be what C came to believe, that image
and likeness, fruit of the illusionist's art, refuse to lighten
the burden of a soul's traffic from one life
into another. *There's a body to be disposed of.*

*

You'd always been a man of parts.
A cut-out figure as you'd say, with a toe-hold
in the thing-world. Entrusting yourself
bit by bit, to the thing-stare: the concentrated look
of a garlic crusher in the manner
of a true Dadaist, "a form of internal mobility"
that lands you in Malta
                   for another look,
running the shade of a finger along the fishtail spirals on
    the walls
falling into line with a cache of bob-haired plank figures,
there's so much to buttonhole
in the afterlife, so much to lean on
and gaze out from, to hold tight and let go of,
dawdling in the crawl-space
                   of a haberdashery,
emporium of trimmings and bobbins,
before bowling past the Silver Horse
and the Smiling Prince (or how about the Still Alive Bar)
all boarded up now in the Gut, where surely you'd sulked,
ever the truant, on your first visit, rubbing shoulders
with the Maltese sailors. Twilit days of '66.
Does anyone have a match?
                 There's a bandaged
manikin behind the vitrine. Is that you
dwelling under your own color? Ink and blood.

*

What of A's vision
of the man arriving

from the west (Sepharad?
his native land and due
west of Comino, which
he'd leave and return to
periodically): On his brow
was a letter blazoned
on each side in blood
and in ink, and the sign
shaped like a baton
between them
was deeply hidden:

The color of the blood
was black and turned red
while the color of the ink
was red and abruptly turned
black and the appearance
of the sign arbitrating
between the two was white.
What is revealed is nothing
short of a miracle for A,
exiled, penniless, denounced
as a heretic for treating
the letters of the Divine
Name as a musical scale
to sound His calling.

And when I caught sight
of his face I took fright,
my heart startled within me
and shifted out of its place
[Job 37:1] and I longed
to speak to call Eldai,
the Sufficient, to help me,
but the thing evaded

my spirit, and when
the man saw my great fear
and the strength of my awe
he opened his mouth
and spoke, and he opened
my mouth to speak

and I answered him
according to his words,
and in my words I turned
into another man, and opened
my eyes and gazed and saw
a fount of seventy tongues
gushing from the letter
on his brow: the sign
on his forehead was called
the potion of death
by the man, but I called it
the potion of life, for what
was dead I turned to life.

*

The gravel road narrows to a cracked defile
snaking down a slope deep in bracken and wild artichoke.
I pick my way along the shoreline, amid boulders

sheared from the cliffside, salt pans and shallows,
the red sands of Ramla bay in the distance, Calypso's cave,
where longing is calibrated in the sea's mood

swings, its lulls and rages, and contrary winds
that claw at its pelt. Bobbing rafts of shearwaters circle
back to their cliff burrows at dusk. A couple

in scuba gear slip under the brine, I imagine
their dumb-show descent, their slow glow-worm trek
in the liquid underworld. Fathom blossoms.

*

Marsalforn. Walk the length of the bay and back before
settling in for two nights at the Lantern Guest House on a
back street of the fishing village rapidly turning into a
resort town. I'm pleased with my tiny, nondescript room
where a shower and toilet are crammed onto the shuttered
balcony with its angled view of clothes-lines and flat
rooftops. I kick off my sandals to give them a break from
sixty kilos of ballast – I'm starting to see things like you,
Silky – hiking to Ramla Bay and then the long, winding
ascent to Ggantija where you'd circled the shrine with
your deadpan stand-in, Costigan, like a pair of old
dowsers, feet dancing out a labyrinth. Flopped on the bed,
I'm instantly asleep. The cat's sick. I take it to the vet who
puts it on a drip. But it only gets thinner, its breathing shal-
lower, and the vet remarks that the cat is malingering and
disconnects it from the life support. It slinks away in per-
fect health. Then a dog trots in and takes a shit in the mid-
dle of my room. Green leaves jumbled in its feces.

*

It's a wonder STC never ventured out
to what Silky came to call "the windings."
Hadn't he spoken while sojourning in Sicily
of childish minds alone attaching themselves
to antiquities? But the slopes of Etna, its crumbling
      aqueducts,
its vineyards and farmhouses, offered a prospect
laminated in the past, while the eerie unfamiliarity

of the megaliths of Malta, their stripped grandeur
could only have perplexed and shaken the poet
into probing their origins. Their bays, half-moons, runaway
spirals and volutes, would have suggested an altogether
different notion of the numinous: earthbound, tuberous,
rooted in flora and herbage, a botanic kingdom of leaf
and tendril, overseen by the softer sex,
his own SH, anagrammed as Asra, a constant
phantom presence that throbbed like the lizard's visible pulse
he'd recorded in his journal that summer.

Then again I'd have thought the shrines mirrored
perfectly the concentricals of his own mind (the very lobes
of the cerebellum), its perturbations and lucidities
its divisions and unity, the enormity of its appetite
its counter-shocks and descending spiral.
      "This Tarantula Dance of repetitious and vertiginous
argumentation in circulo, begun in imposture & [self]
consummated in madness."
                              Stepping through doorways
like portholes, into the grooved and pitted, ochre-
washed chamber of dreams, here, at the Mediterranean's
dead center, latitude/longitude 35° 50' N, 14° 35' E
in a long, candy-colored afterglow
of the dying hour I recall wandering in a vast warehouse
half-lost, fearful yet curious, straying deeper into its tangle
of passageways, where a performance is taking place,

real & spectral at the same moment – I can't be sure,
one set of people, initiates like myself are being stalked,
shot at with arrows that kill or freeze us into place,
and I'm stark naked, but snatch a pair of pants from a rack
as I wander upstairs where someone spots me
and gives chase, and I swiftly slide behind one door
after another, until I end up squeezed in a closet

from where I can hear laughter from the other side
of the wall, merry-making, I even imagine
hearing a familiar voice, and it strikes me I've stumbled
upon the opening of an art show, a vernissage,
as I slip out, relieved, keeping a low profile.

*

Lay it down   in a line of ink   like the bricklayer's
art a half-brick over   a whole brick and a whole
brick over   a half-brick   a line of life
image and likeness   moving in two paths the way
of a ship   in the heart   of the seas
leaving no trace to   sing on the breath (hadn't I
jotted down   en route to Malta   the exact words
from an in-flight   magazine)   maintaining
a steady   flow of air letting   the voice float
on it I read buckled   to my seat minutes before
landing as   the island swung   into view

on the other hand   to sing in the mask
is a term   that would have pleased   you Silky
with your debonair   Double lighting out
for *the easy   breath of the Levant* focusing   your voice till
you feel it resound   in the nasal region
O Geppetto   O Pinocchio tangled   in the strings
of the all-too-human   you who'd whittled
the self to   a line of ink a line   of blood
knock-kneed pigeon   toed with the button-
hole stare   of a tailor's dummy   this is your
cue Silky this is where   you throw your voice
                    at the living

*

Back in Valletta I unpack, head straight
for the Oratory. It's been two weeks since I stood
in front of *The Beheading,* and I'm curious
to note the effect of seeing again the painting
I had revisited in my own mind
while on Gozo. An elderly couple scans the canvas
with an opera glass handed back and forth
as they pick out the figures draped in the somber colors
of their vigil, before fixing the glass on the dark
that shudders down the first martyr's spine –
C's *semblable* – as he's brought low, the bare outline
of an animal pelt protruding from under the folds
of his scarlet robe, a reminder of his origins,
Jehohanan, "YHWH is gracious," who fed on locusts
and wild honey, and yet C's sympathy extends
to the entire ensemble in its unknowing, this is the lesson
I draw for myself shifting my attention
for a split second from the painting to its image reduced
to pixels in a cell phone raised toward the canvas,
this, and the broader realization that for all its manifest
naturalism *The Beheading* is best glossed in the eclipse
of its own light, for within the short span of time
left to C, the act of painting would form a mystic
counterpoint to the wreckage of his life,
as though in this last dim cluster of spectral enactments
C had broken the surface of his own gaze
and could barely sustain the fixed stare
of the almost human. Having fled Malta,
convinced there was still a price on his head,
C must have sought refuge, if not salvation
in images of Decapitation, Burial, Adoration,
Resurrection, executed while adrift in Sicily,
for he was floundering (his face horribly disfigured
in a Neapolitan tavern) and coming up for air
with each brushstroke applied to canvas was,

in a sense, a form of baptism, of immersion
in the pure medium of his sight, hence the searing irony
of his final days, when officially pardoned
he'd set out for Rome in a felucca, only to be collared
in the port of Palo Romano by an overzealous
customs officer who mistook him for someone else.
By the time the error was righted the felucca
had set sail, along with his rolled canvases,
among them one last version of a young-looking,
melancholic St. John, The Forerunner.
The reports may be exaggerated, but according
to Baglione, C tramped along the beach
under a hot July sun in pursuit of the missing
vessel, and, contracting a fever, died
within days "as miserably as he had lived."

*

We're a motley crew dragging our feet down
    the storied chambers, "Watch your step,"
        our guide keeps shouting over his shoulder

in a whisper, "Keep your heads low,"
    as we peer down the spiraling passageway
        and shuffle on toward the oracle

room, "Seven steps down leading nowhere,"
    our guide again, raising the ante, step by step,
        deeper down, until pressed into a knot

at the lowest level, we're ready to hear Echo
    resound like a hi-fi in our ears, just some scraps
        of air escaping from the lungs,

but in the underworld things get blown
    out of proportion, and we imagine unheard
        meanings in the sounds, like A

playing havoc with the alphabet, or you, Silky,
    beating a retreat to Malta, with your petitioner
        of spirals, your shadowy semblance,

like one pulled down by the Sleeping Lady
    to a greater intensity, among all the knobby
        ex votos, the flints and pendants,

and dripstone heads, she winds you home.

                        *

Glass-encased manuscripts line the walls in the museum
next to the Mdina Cathedral, but what catches the eye is
an impressive display of grainy photographs of Dun Karm,
the national poet in his priest's soutane, feeding his
beloved canary in its wicker cage, sitting sternly at his roll-
top desk, visiting schoolchildren. His resemblance to you,
Silky, is uncanny. The same high forehead and long, dour
face offset by Groucho eyes. The day before my departure
I decide to visit the National Library, a baroque affair
embellished by the long arm of Empire and once the
home of the last Knight on the island, who would
bequeath to the city his palace and its massive, antique
library. I am escorted to my seat and within minutes the
librarian returns with my request, a collection of Dun
Karm's poems, which are largely religious in nature. Even
when filtered down in mothball English, more darkness
than light shows through the fabric of words. But I strug-
gle on and alight on a poem to his songbird, how it would
drop the sweetest notes into his ear each morning, before

he shuffled out of his tiny apartment and turned the key in
the lock behind him.

*

My little pinball pet bouncing
off the corners of my soutane,

my Maltese ox-eye in the first sprinkle
of light over the Grand Harbor

and all its nifty boats clipping
the wavelets, it is to you I scratch

my doleful poems in the Biblio-
theca, to you I address my reveries

as you poke your peppercorn head
out from under your pinfeathers, I am

a sad-sack priest with a face
as long as the dry-dock cranes,

call me your undervoice,
the dumbwaiter of your song's ascent.

The Mu'allaqa
of Imru al-Qays

THE MU'ALLAQA OF IMRU AL-QAYS

Rein in your mares and weep, for a love and a campsite
    at the dune's twisted edge between al-Dakhul and Haumal,
Toodih and al-Mikrat, whose traces haven't yet been swept
                                              away
    by the weavings of the southern and northerly winds,
and look at the doe droppings scattered like peppercorns
    in the sandhollows and beds of gravel.
                                The morning
they bundled their belongings by the thorny acacia and left
    I felt as if I'd sunk my teeth into a gourd.
Holding their riding-beasts back, my companions said,
    "Come, be patient, don't wallow in grief,"
while tears were my only solace, for is there anything
    to lean on in this trackless halting-place?
Wasn't it the same before her? First came Umm al-Hawarith,
    and then her neighbor al-Rabab, from Ma'sal.
Musk drifted from their bodies like the breath
    of the east wind, pungent with cloves.
More tears of longing welled up and started to trickle
    down and streak the strap of my sword.

Many a fine day I've had and can't help thinking
    of the time at Dara Juljul I hacked my she-camel
for a couple of young girls, saddlebags sagging with goods,
    and they tossed choice cuts back and forth,
the fat twisting into tassels of silk. Or what
    of the time I stole into the howdah
hiding Unayza, and she cried, "You bastard, let me out,
    I'll follow on foot," and when the litter tilted
she cried even louder, "You're crippling my camel!"
    And I cried back, "Go on, slacken the reins,
and don't think you can keep me from plucking your fruit!"

I've sneaked at night into many a tent
of women with child, and mothers suckling their infants,
    and I've steered their hearts from their darlings
covered in amulets. And when the babe started to bawl
    she'd twist half of her body his way, and leave
the other half for me. But another time she fled
    down the dune and swore we were done.
                                        "Easy
Fatima, and cut the scorn, if you're bent on leaving me
    do it gently. And if I've annoyed you, sort my clothes
from yours for good. Emboldened by this folly
    that's killing me, you know I'm at your beck and call,
and your eyes dissolve in tears only to let their arrows
    pierce the remains of a slain heart."

                        *

Then there was Bayda, cloistered in her shell.
    I had her too, after I'd skirted the tribesmen
who'd boasted they'd kill me. The Pleiades had just risen
    and gleamed like gemmed fringes on a sash
when I entered, and she shivered behind the divider,
    her clothes there in a heap beside her, except
for her shift. "By Allah, you won't get away with this!"
    she cried, as I egged her on and she swept
our tracks clean with the edge of her brocaded gown.
    We crossed the campground and dropped
out of sight in the ribbed hollow of a giant dune,
    and when I parted her braids, she leaned forward –
slender-hipped, firm-ankled, slim, egg-white,
    her abdomen flat and breast-bones
buffed like a burnished mirror – and shying back
    revealed the softest cheek, the glance
of a Wajra gazelle with its fawn, and an antelope's
    neck, neither uncomely nor unadorned

when raised in full view, and the dark shock of her hair
    curled down her back like clusters of dates
(while her upswept locks were plaited with threads
    lost in a tangle of loosened strands)
and a waist as small as a camel's nose-ring,
    and a shinbone lean as the stalk of a papyrus.
Mornings, crumbs of musk are scattered on her bed
    where she languishes till noon, not bothering
to slip on a gown or sash, and the fingers she raises
    are not coarse, but soft as the sandworms
of Zaby, or tamarisk toothpicks, and evenings
    she illumines the dark as though she were a light
to a hermit at his devotions. On the like of her
    the wise gaze with fervor as she flaunts
her curves in a dress midway between a child's frock
    and a woman's robe. Fresh as an ostrich's
yellow-speckled egg, nourished by unsullied water.
    Other men's follies divert their passions
but my heart won't swerve from loving her,
    and many a pigheaded rival I've repulsed,
sincere, disapproving types, never short of advice.

*

Ah, many a night has draped its curtains over me
    like the billows of the sea, weighed down with cares,
it has tried my strength. And when it stretched its haunches
    and raised its rump before heaving its chest, "By God,"
I said, "sluggish night, give way to morning, though surely
    daybreak is no better than you! What a night
you are, with your legion of stars roped to Yadhbul's
    summit and the Pleiades fixed in place
by flax twined to solid rock."
                Many a friend's waterskin
    I've slung over my shoulders, humble, cumbered

with my gear, and I've trekked across many a wadi
    bare as the belly of a wild ass, where the lean wolf howls
like an outcast grubbing for scraps. And I said to him
    when he finished his howling, "Aren't we a pair,
the two of us hard up, living on air, and when something
                                      comes
    our way, it slips through our fingers; scavengers
will find scant pickings on your parcel of land, or mine."

*

Often I've set out in the morning, birds still in their nests,
    on a smooth-coated outstripper of wild game,
charging, wheeling round, pressing forward, then back in
                                     a flash,
    like a boulder crashing down in the grip of a torrent,
a dark bay, its saddle-cloth sliding off its back
    as smooth stones make for a slippery hold.
Though lean, he's all pluck and ardor set to boil
    in his neighing like a seething cauldron,
                           headlong he flows,
while mares falling behind kick up dust
    on the flattened badlands; the featherweight
boy slips from his back, and bucking he flings off
    the rough-rider caught in the folds of his own robe,
swift as a spinning top whirled from a child's hand
    with a knotted string; as the flanks of a gazelle,
the legs of an ostrich, a wolf's dash, and fox's lope;
    with his streamlined frame you can see
from behind a bushy tail barely touching the ground
    that bars the gap between his hind legs.
Standing beside the tent, his back seems slick
    as a grinding stone for a bride's balms,
or a slab for splitting the rind of a gourd.
                                 Bloodflecks

spatter over his neck from the head of the flock –
juice of the henna plant streaked through strands
    of gray hair – while a herd of oryx swinging
into view look like girls from Duwar in long robes
    and, swirling round, resemble beads of light
and dark onyx on the neck of a purebred boy.
    He thrusts me ahead before a clutch of stragglers
has a chance to disperse, then shoots forward,
    breasting his way between a buck and a doe,
in constant motion, neither sprinkled nor soaked in sweat.
    And the cooks are put to work, some poking
at the cuts on the grill, while others hastily
    stir the stew in a pot, and returning at dusk,
our gaze can scarcely take him in, for the raised eye
    is swiftly lowered. All night long he stands
where I can see him, saddled and bridled, not cut loose.

                    *

My friend, can you see the faint bolt of lightning?
    Look how it flashes in the distance like a flicker
of hands in the thunderhead crowning the skies.
    It flares with the brilliance of lamps whose wicks
a recluse has twisted and dipped in oil.
    I sat with my companions between Darij
and al-Udhayb, gazing out into the desert fastness.
    We reckoned its downpour had swept over Qatan
on our right, even as it drummed down to the left
    over al-Sitar and far off Yadhbul.
                            Then it unloosed
its load over Kutayfa, and thrashed the thorn trees
    to the ground, as sheets of rain spreading over al-Qanan
drove the white-hoofed ibex from every nook and ledge.
    Not a single palm was left standing in Tayma,
nor any building, save a stone fort;

and when the rains gathered force, Thabir
resembled an old chief bundled in a striped cloak,
    while the early morning peaks of al-Mujaymir,
scored with debris, looked like the whirl
    of a spindle.
                         The cloudburst released its waters
over the wastes of al-Ghabit like a Yemeni unloading
    his bag of goods for sale, and at daybreak the finches
in the broad wadi were giddy with spiced wine,
    while beasts of prey at dusk, drowned in the furthest
                                  reaches,
lay stiff on their sides like uprooted bulbs of squill.

Hermetica

THE HOUSE OF LEONTIS

Be remembered for good and for praise, Kyrios
    Leontis, who paved his home in iridescent
stone and glass, the siren's eyes bearing a curious
    resemblance to those of the man bound
to the mast with a fish-net.
                         Friends called him Kloubas,
    "birdcage," suggesting sundry meanings
contracted to a shorthand reserved
    for soul-mates, while I'm left to myself in the open-air
remains of his home, gazing across the Jordan
    Valley Rift at a sudden flock of crested fowl
joy-riding the thermals above the beaten earth
    floor he tesserated at his own expense –
the allure of the songstress, greenish hair
    loosened on bare shoulders, is his own doubtful
salvation as her flute startles a poorly
    preserved passerine – brittle, colored bits
of its plumage long missing – into flight.

INTAGLIO

Chip of a coin, picked up with the quick and eager eye
of a child – finders keepers, kicking dust

beneath no palm where sad Judaea weeps.
Oxide coated disk, finely brushed,

soaked in lemon, and dried.
For weeks we turned you over in vain

between thumb and forefinger
before you emerged as from dark waters, a somber

profile with heavy brows, and the wraith
of a wreath for a crown. Scant viridescent held gingerly

in the morning light, struck from what crude die?
Grim, peppercorn king, come up for air.

HERMETICA

Imagine each page of the book a fire-breathing
specter, and you, following ponderously
behind, reading between the lines.
Stop dragging your heels the blue flame rasps into the gap:
surely this is the mind of sovereignty
speaking – the divine rag of a voice snatched
from no man's jaws.
                              "But tell me once more about the way up,"
you plead to the three times great (if only
it mattered): ibis, or baboon, a god that laughs
the world into being. Raising your eyes from the book
that rests on your lap, you gaze out at indigo skies
and pay heed to the kestrels, crying kyrie kyrie
in their coming and going.

                    *

Take the words out of your mouth
(Trismegistus again) *and sow them under the tread of your feet*
where lupin flaunt their inflorescence
in a field of mustard. And though the mind is glimpsed
in the act of understanding,
                              ignorance dogs
my steps, even here in the open air,
wading through waist-high grasses, musk-dead
nettle and scrub. The hillside contracts
for a split second through the pinhole of the pupil.
On hands and knees I summon up
the name of the shyest of plants, the low-lying
star of Bethlehem.

I took the hollyhock for a friend,
monocled and lank as royalty, by the disused tracks.
Now you see me and now you don't,
that's what I said under my breath
as I ran by its flying colors.
Wild oat panicles scattered the contents
of their papery purses to the wind,

                            as if they too spoke
their mind in the simplest of gestures –
but I ran on, joyfully lapping up the years,
two, three crossties at a time, feet pounding the earth,
this poor bedding of detritus, whose core
spews fire, this gored mantle rock
absorbing my shadow.

                *

You read how an image of the good
might draw you up as a magnet draws iron,
and though the *Corpus* is unequivocal
on the matter, you're left more baffled than ever
as you step outside, dodging
the loony fruit bats' skittery orbits
in the penumbra, sonneteers

                        of no sound
plumbed but an airy solace;
– at this hour the mind drifts benevolently
in sublunary gloss and stress,
in brief, cursive flights of sudden voyance,
and for a moment you could swear
nothing was beyond redress.

GADARA

I'd been counting, short of breath, the bright
    knobs of the mountain-rambling thistles when
we crossed paths, and he who kindles the fire, the boy-
    archer, lurked in your eyes, 'It's a bit hard

on the knees, the descent,' you said – then you were gone,
    even as I turned to answer, so I walked on
to the ruined city on the high spur, overlooking the sea
    of Galilee incandescent as the devil's tongue.

ÆGEAN

Not a white, insists Simonides, but crimson
sail, dyed with the moist berry

of the holm-oak and hoisted in sight of landfall,
should the boy return in one piece –

but Ægeus clapped eyes on a tarred
canvas as the craft plied home, and grief raveled

its ball of twine across the archipelagoes,
back to the tangled dance

in the House of the Double Axe,
back to a thousand riffs on the panpipe, as he leapt –

naturalized, tasting the salt on his sleeve
even before impact,

slipping like a conjuror behind the brooding
mirror that bears his name.

IN ELEA

after Parmenides

This plenum rooted in water
where I plant my feet firmly in the air
and listen to the wind as it frisks

the fronds of the date palm
in the courtyard, the sound of equivalences
undivided and imperishable;

soon the dark, material
illusionist will rise over these hills –
oh shadow playing moon,
what lies beyond

is lassoed in where the sea
champs at the bit, mares on the trail
sense, come to carry me as far
as desire might reach.

HERMES

How many years since my fingers
struck the shadowed keys. The punch-drunk
gradient on which to scrape a living
as the clipped gait of the carriage
rings at the end of the line, you know
the saying: *if the heart races ahead,*
turn back. Night watchman, thief

at the high gates, what lurks behind
begins to seep through the chassis
and its hard-pressed letters thumped
vibrant as the strings on your newfound toy,
scooped out from the live marrow
of the turtle shell: such ominous sounds,
random song in the mottled light.

WHEN DAYS RUN ON MONOTONOUSLY

From the Visions of the Latter-day Prophets

AFTER H. N. BIALIK

When days run on monotonously, year in and year out,
each the same as yesterday and the day before,
mere days, of small comfort and much tedium,
and lassitude strikes man and beast alike,
a man sets out at sunset to stroll along the shore,
he notes that the sea hasn't fled,
and yawns;
he ventures out to the Jordan that hasn't retreated,
and yawns;
he looks up at the Pleiades and Orion that haven't budged,
and yawns.
Man and beast hunch together, bored –
their lives weigh heavily upon them;
desolation plucks at the hairs of every man's head,
the cat loses its whiskers.

Then longings surge.
They mushroom like fungus raising a stink
on a decaying wood plank.
The cracks and crevices fill with longings
like rags infested with lice.
A man returns to his lodgings for supper,
dips his crust and herring in vinegar –
and longs;
he drinks from his murky, lukewarm cup –
and longs;
he removes shoes and socks by the edge of the bed –
and longs.
Man and beast hunch together, longing.
In his dreams man moans from unabated longings,

a cat on a tin roof pules and claws.
Then hunger gnaws.
Devouring, wondrous, unrivalled.
Neither for bread nor visions, but the Messiah.

In the pre-dawn chill before sunrise,
confined to his bed, in the room of his lodgings,
riddled with insomnia, dream-glutted,
empty of spirit, man stirs awake (webs of vexed sleep
gummed to his eyelids, the dread of night
in his bones, and the cat still caterwauling,
clawing at his brain-tissue and nerves)
and shuffles to the window to wipe off the steam;
or, standing by the open door, shades
his bleary, jaundiced eyes with his hands,
and stares, hungry for salvation,
at the footpath beyond the yard,
at the rubbish heap facing his home –
seeking the Messiah.
And kicking off the blankets, his wife rises,
grim-faced, disheveled, her body
worn to the bone, she jerks a shriveled pap
from her infant's mouth, and listens, intently:
is that the Messiah coming?
Wasn't that the braying of his donkey?
The infant peers over his crib,
the mouse peeps out of its hole:
is that the Messiah coming?
Wasn't that the jingling of bells on his donkey?
The maid fanning the samovar behind the stove
sticks out her coal-black face:
is that the Messiah coming?
Isn't that the blast of his horn?

(1908)

SULTAN ACHMED HAIKU

How the years cry out
the sounds of their unmaking.
The dirt poor whirl round

our startled bodies
and vanish, our pockets de-
pleted by fingers

light as the seagulls,
seamstresses snipping the air
above the slender-

waisted minarets:
the Blue Mosque of my being,
desire's sweet lift off.

JEROME

for Shimon Sandbank

Walled in by the desert, he had no patience
for the solitary rigors of monks in rags
and, notwithstanding the brushwork of pinched
flesh-tints (the wasting away and slag
of self-immolation) displayed on canvas and panel,
the barometer of his affections drew him
elsewhere and turned him into a pupil
of Hebrew, "this language of hissing and grim
aspirates." But I see him as Antonello
da Messina – who brought to Venice the secrets
of oil glazing – saw him: in the airiness
of his study, where the play of light mellows
chapter and verse propped on his desk,
on which he trains his mind in muted bliss.
– He who'd pleaded, "Step out, I beg you, a little
from your body," scrapes back his chair
and treads three steps down, while the peaceable
lion pads in the cloister with nowhere
to go, lost in a perspective that fools the eyes
and bids the heart to linger in the domed
mansion, at noon-tide, amid the cries
of swifts, glimpsed through the high windows,
seeding the air. To live and move
under the veritable Bethlehem skies, and *thrust
the hand into the flame* translating the Good
Book for everyman, and day by day to prove
how words might heave and break the crust,
the hard Judean soil, and serve as food.

THROUGH THE DESERT

For weeks I'd dreamt of the desert castle circuit.
Names bitter as the bitter gourd, Hallabat,
lush Azraq with its high water table,
the crumbling black basalt of al-Kharaneh,
and in the midst of the scabland
a crush of figures confected on the walls of Qusayr Amra:
bathhouse, hunting lodge, minuscule
pleasure dome and retreat for what Damascene prince
corralled in the city? The pocked surfaces
tell more than their despoilers intended
to conceal in the looping hook-and-eye script
that spiders across the pageantry.
                              How then to consign
such images to the retreat of our own
timid minds? We who are passing through
and have come out of the heat, where the sun
ossifies the desert shrubs, now move
clockwise in the cool chamber, outstared
by pride of another age we might not
have imagined east of the Jordan.

§

A man digs for water. He loosens the cords
of his home pitched only yesterday, and a woman
ravels her belongings with the foreknowledge
in her hands of other journeys – after the boundary
marking and cairn-raising, the striking down
and setting out, and the cracked voices
of children hooting at the hobbled camel-herd for the trek
from station to station:

                              one scours the dry
watercourse, another sparks
the root-net tinder of white broom,
while a third stirs the embers, delving for spirits
who won't release their hold on the mind.
Smoke of the henna. Listen. The sputter-and-click
of withering flames under the New Moon
of Ripe-Grain. Vocatives quick on the tongue.
Then the letting go ...

                    §

    The nib you gripped to scratch some lines
on stone came from a two-by-four
flung into the fire.
                        It's all you retrieved
from the ashes raked at sunrise,
an old nail that held for dear life
some boards together, so why not leave behind
a straggle of words for the devil knows
who to chew over in the sun – you imagined the loess
plain and its abrupt
outcroppings
a vast escritoire, and circling back
months later to the same makeshift camp,
half-expected to find someone else's
wayward graffiti appended to your own
on the rockface where two rams
lock horns –
                    the north wind
has bitten your flesh to the bone, *a man*
is nothing but what he tells
his self to be,
                    dutifully jotted down among gleanings

you will name the *Ghuraba,* The Book
of Strangers.

§

   Pitched into the dry plain, a flurry of quarter-tones
set free from white deal and clinched
in the ear before giving me the slip,
like the crisscrossing fennel fox tracks luring me away
from the village. Scrambling up loose shale
in the box canyon. Wormwood and groundsel,
and the common sparrow rouged from nesting in the
      scalloped face
of the sandstone cliffs.
                              The eagle's feather
plucks the double strings,
till sounds wrinkle into the wisest face.
Here is the blue tongue of air and fire in the live wood,
the houri's dance kneaded from earth
and water − a cache of flourishes
rising from the soundboard, and borne
on the wind.
                        (Come nightfall
young Hisham thrums on the oud
in Wadi Rumm, by the ruins of the temple
of the goddess Allat.)

§

Come March, come April, red stonecrop
underfoot, sprung on the sly,
                              dwarf and succulent −
a scribble of flora
parading their passing: catmint

and oxeye, and further afield the profitless acacia
quicken the soul slumped in the saddle
as words after silence puddle into a song of all
our vanishings, and the promise
softly coaxed out of seasonal journeyings
on the desert circuit.

ENVOI

So say farewell to the figure curled in the ashcan
bobbing on the sea, somebody's dead ringer,
though you can't put your finger on who it might be,
wave goodbye as the current sweeps the makeshift
bark past Veer Point and into the main —
it's the journey out now, for the Soother of Absence.
"Catch you later!" he'd shout back, if he hadn't made himself scarce,
the mooning semblance who's dogged your steps
is drifting elsewhere, it's cozy in his think-tank berth,
the fire in his eyes banked, dozing under
a pile of leaves, he's coiled tight as a colophon.

NOTES

THE MALTESE DREAMBOOK, *page* 29 *ff*

A   Avraham Abulafia. There is strong evidence to suggest that the Saragossa-born Hebrew Cabbalist sought refuge on the tiny island of Comino from 1285–88.

C   Michelangelo Merisi da Caravaggio. Escaped to Malta in 1607 where he was admitted into the Order of St. John only to be defrocked (in absentia) after he came to blows with a knight and fled the island.

STC   Samuel Taylor Coleridge landed in Valletta May 18, 1804 and remained in Malta for just over a year.

Silky   Dennis Silk. London-born poet and originator of Thing Theater, which he practiced in Jerusalem, his adopted city from 1955. He sojourned in Malta for several months in 1966 where he worked on his short fiction *Costigan.*

THE MU'ALLAQA OF IMRU AL-QAYS, *page* 53 *ff*

Imru al-Qays, the Vagabond Prince of the Kinda tribe of central Arabia, also known as the Creator of Images, lived in the mid-sixth century AD and is generally considered the most distinguished and influential of the pre-Islamic poets. His qasida opens the *Mu'allaqat,* a collection of odes – traditionally believed to have been hung on *(mu'allaqa)* the Ka'ba as prize poems during the annual fair at Ukaz – authored by seven remarkable Arabian poets and compiled in the eighth century by the legendary Hammad al-Rawia, last of the true *rawis,* or reciters of oral tribal poetry.